Greater Than a Tourist Book Series Reviews from Readers

I think the series is wonderful and beneficial for tourists to get information before visiting the city.

-Seckin Zumbul, Izmir, Turkey

I am a world traveler who has read many trip guides but this one really made a difference for me. I would call it a heartfelt creation of a local guide expert instead of just a guide.

-Susy, Isla Holbox, Mexico

New to the area like me, this is a must have!

-Joe, Bloomington, USA

This is a good series that gets down to it when looking for things to do at your destination without having to read a novel for just a few ideas.

-Rachel, Monterey, USA

Good information to have to plan my trip to this destination.

-Pennie Farrell, Mexico

Great ideas for a port day.

-Mary Martin, USA

Aptly titled, you won't just be a tourist after reading this book. You'll be greater than a tourist!

-Alan Warner, Grand Rapids, USA

Even though I only have three days to spend in San Miguel in an upcoming visit, I will use the author's suggestions to guide some of my time there. An easy read - with chapters named to guide me in directions I want to go.

-Robert Catapano, USA

Great insights from a local perspective! Useful information and a very good value!

-Sarah, USA

This series provides an in-depth experience through the eyes of a local. Reading these series will help you to travel the city in with confidence and it'll make your journey a unique one.

-Andrew Teoh, Ipoh, Malaysia

GREATER THAN A TOURIST-
CHARLOTTESVILLE
VIRGINIA
USA

50+ Travel Tips from a Local

Reed Willard

CZYK Publishing Since 2011.
CZYKPublishing.com
Greater Than a Tourist

Mill Hall, PA
All rights reserved.
ISBN: 9798353983484

>TOURIST

50 TRAVEL TIPS FROM A LOCAL

BOOK DESCRIPTION

With travel tips and culture in our guidebooks written by a local, it is never too late to visit Charlottesville. Greater Than a Tourist- Charlottesville, Virginia, USA, by Reed Willard offers the inside scoop on Wahoo Country. Most travel books tell you how to travel like a tourist. While there is nothing wrong with that, as part of the 'Greater Than a Tourist' series, this book will give you candid travel tips from someone who has lived at your next travel destination. This guidebook will not tell you exact addresses or store hours but instead gives you knowledge that you may not find in other travel books. Experience cultural, culinary delights, and attractions with the guidance of a local. Slow down and get to know the people with this invaluable guide. By the time you finish this book, you will be eager and prepared to discover new activities at your next travel destination.

Inside this guidebook, you will find:

Visitor information from a Local
Tour ideas and inspiration
Valuable guidebook information

Greater Than a Tourist- A Travel Guidebook with 50+ Travel Tips from a Local. Slow down, stay in one place, and get to know the people and culture. By the time you finish this book, you will be eager and prepared to travel to your next destination.

OUR STORY

Traveling is a passion of the Greater than a Tourist book series creator. Lisa studied abroad in college, and for their honeymoon, Lisa and her husband toured Europe. During her travels through Malta, an older man tried to give her some advice based on his own experience living on the island since he was a young boy. She was not sure if she should talk to the stranger but was interested in his advice. When traveling to some places, she was wary to talk to locals because she was afraid that they weren't being genuine. Through her travels, Lisa learned how much locals had to share with tourists. Lisa created the Greater Than a Tourist book series to help connect people with locals. A topic that locals are very passionate about sharing.

TABLE OF CONTENTS

Summer Activities

11. Kayaking, Canoeing, or Tubing Down the Rivanna River
12. The Shenandoah National Park
13. Fishing and Swimming at a Public Lake
14. Public Pools
15. Polo Matches
16. The Skate Park

Fall Activities

17. Apple Picking on Carter Mountain
18. Leaf Peeping on the Skyline Drive
19. Epic Autumn Hikes
20. Wine Tasting and Vineyard Tours
21. The Montpelier Hunt Races
22. Trick-or-Treating on the Lawn

Winter Activities

23. Skiing/Snowboarding at Wintergreen
24. Massanutten
25. Lighting of the Lawn
26. Charlottesville's Grand Illumination
27. The Holiday Market
28. First Night Virginia

Where to Stay

44. Keswick Hall
45. Boar's Head Resort
46. Oakhurst Inn
47. The Clifton

Entertainment & Nightlife

48. Fridays After Five & The Ting Pavilion
49. Breweries and The Charlottesville Ale Trail
50. The Downtown Mall (Jefferson and Paramount Theaters)
51. Virginia Theatre Festival

Bonus Tips: Day Trips

52. Richmond
53. Washington D.C.
54. Virginia Beach
55. The Historic Triangle (Jamestown, Colonial Williamsburg, and Yorktown)
56. Theme Parks (Busch Gardens, Water Country USA, and King's Dominion)
57. Luray Caverns

AUTHOR'S DEDICATION

This book is dedicated to the fiercest Wahoo I know, my mother.

And to my wife and our beautiful daughter Amelia - I cannot wait to explore my hometown with you both and "tick-tick" every activity mentioned in this guide.

ABOUT THE AUTHOR

Reed Willard is a writer, actor, and performer who lives with his wife and young daughter, Melly.

Although he has lived in almost a dozen cities around the world, Reed is proud to call Virginia home. He was born and raised in Charlottesville, VA, before heading over the mountain to Harrisonburg where he attended James Madison University.

After graduating in 2006 with a degree in Communication Studies, Reed packed up and moved out west as an aspiring actor. After a few years of grinding and hustling, Reed began experiencing modest success in small TV roles and commercials, as well as leading roles in professional theatre

3

productions. He also began writing, both as a creative travel blogger and as a playwright.

In 2015, Reed put acting and writing on hold to pursue a lifelong dream of thru-hiking the entire Appalachian Trail (Georgia to Maine, 2,189 miles). He set off on April 7, 2015, and completed the epic journey five and a half months later. After that, he continued traveling, working jobs on sailing boats and luxury cruise ships in Hawaii and Alaska respectively, before settling in Chicago to resume his acting career.

After a year and a half of performing in regional theatres throughout Chicago, Reed landed a role in *The Wizarding World of Harry Potter* at Universal Studios Japan in 2018. He lived and performed in Osaka for a year before switching gears and becoming the main villain, Deacon, in the *Waterworld* stunt show at Universal Studios Singapore.

Then in 2020, the Covid-19 pandemic arrived bringing everything to a halt. But not for Reed. In the middle of the raging pandemic, Reed's first child Amelia "Melly" was born in Singapore. He also married his wife Khezz before being forced to leave due to the crisis. Fortunately, he was not away from his wife and child for long and was able to reunite with them in Manila by Christmas that year.

Since then, Reed has switched gears yet again and started working full-time as a freelance writer and editor. *Greater Than a Tourist - Charlottesville* marks Reed's first published book - the first of many, he promises. And he can't wait to return to his hometown, wife and child in tow, to show them all of the wonderful things that Charlottesville has to offer.

HOW TO USE THIS BOOK

Each *Greater Than a Tourist* book is written by someone who has lived in an area for over three months. The goal of this book is to help travelers prepare for and experience different locations by providing opinions from a local. The author has made suggestions based on their own experiences. Please check before traveling to the area in case the suggested places are unavailable.

Travel Advisories: As a first step in planning any trip abroad, check the Travel Advisories for your intended destination.
https://travel.state.gov/content/travel/en/traveladvisories/traveladvisories.html

FROM THE PUBLISHER

Traveling can be one of the most important parts of a person's life. The excitement and memories that you have are some of the best. As the publisher of the Greater Than a Tourist series, as well as the popular *50 Things to Know* book series, we strive to help you learn about new places, spark your imagination, and inspire you. Wherever you are and whatever you do, I wish you safe, fun, and inspiring travel.

Lisa Rusczyk Ed. D.
CZYK Publishing

"Tourists don't know where they've been, travelers don't know where they're going."

- Paul Theroux

Charlottesville, or "C-ville" to the locals, has a little something for everyone. Whether you're a history buff, a sports fan, an aspiring artist, or simply a newlywed couple looking for a nice place to start a family, Charlottesville may be the place for you. After all, there's a reason that it consistently ranks as one of the best cities in the US to live in and has been lauded through the years as everything from "America's Happiest City" to "Country's Best Mountain Town."

While it has grown a lot in recent years, C-ville still maintains that friendly small-town vibe that is both welcoming and charming to everyone that visits. Located in the heart of Virginia and surrounded by the majestic Blue Ridge Mountains, Charlottesville offers you the opportunity to be in the wilderness in a matter of minutes but is also close enough to the ocean for a quick weekend getaway. It is a city steeped in history, with a thriving music and art scene, a booming wine industry, and a selection of eateries that attract foodies from across the state. No matter what time of year you visit, there are always a ton of activities for both adults and children, and the world-class accommodations in the area are second to none. Then again, there's no need to take my word for it - go see for yourself! And this guidebook will help you do just that. Enjoy!

WAHOOWA

1. UVA

One name that you will see mentioned a lot throughout this travel guide is Thomas Jefferson. He was quite a busy man and his resume boasts more than a few accomplishments; you know, things like authoring the Declaration of Independence and becoming the third President of the United States. He also found the time in his busy schedule to establish the University of Virginia (UVA) in 1819. He envisioned an "academic village" where students could come from all over the blossoming US and "drink of the cup of knowledge."

Today, UVA hosts more than 25,000 students and is considered one of the top public universities in the nation. Its list of alumni includes names like Edgar Allen Poe, Woodrow Wilson, Robert and Ted Kennedy, Katie Couric, David Baldacci, Tina Fey, Ralph Sampson, and the Barber brothers (Tiki and Ronde). It boasts a large academic medical center, with several departments that are nationally recognized and respected. It also has one of the best sports programs of any university in the country, and the university campus - excuse me, I mean the university *grounds* - is listed as a UNESCO World Heritage Site. This brings me to another point: the university has its own lingo. The campus is called "the grounds." Students are referred to as first, second, third, or fourth years rather than freshman, sophomore, etc. And collectively, all students and alumni are known as "Wahoos." More on that last term next.

2. WHAT THE HECK IS A WAHOO?

While the official UVA mascot is the Cavalier, somewhere along the line, fish got involved and now UVA fans lovingly refer to each other as "Wahoos" or just 'Hoos.

So, where did it all begin? Well, legend has it that a bitter sports rivalry existed between UVA and Washington and Lee University in the late nineteenth century. The latter's fans dubbed the UVA crowd as a bunch of "wahoos;" an obvious snub regarding their bawdy and uncouth behavior. Surprisingly, the rowdy bunch took to the moniker and it has remained ever since. Today, the nickname is stronger than ever and some students may claim that they have more in common with the wahoo fish - one that can drink twice its body weight. Whatever the case, the fact remains that "the UVA Cavaliers" is only used in formal discussion. Otherwise, it's "Go Hoos!" *Note: The rivalry that existed with Washington and Lee has long since faded. Today, the Hoos' archrival is undoubtedly the Virginia Tech Hokies.*

3. THE ROTUNDA AND LAWN

The Rotunda is the centerpiece of Jefferson's Academic Village and is modeled after the Pantheon in Rome. A culturally impressive building, it was designed to represent the "authority in nature and power of reason." And that it does! Its original function was that of a library but it is now used as an academic study hall and to host important events, while inspiring greatness in the Wahoos that pass by it.

The Rotunda on UVA's Grounds

At its feet is the **Lawn**. Not to be confused with any regular college quad, the Lawn was part of Jefferson's grand design and is where students and locals alike now go to relax, study, or throw a frisbee. On either side of the Lawn are ten Pavilions and 54 Lawn Rooms. Each Pavilion houses one faculty member and their family on the upper two floors, while the ground floor is used to teach. The 54 Lawn Rooms are given to carefully selected fourth-year undergrads who excel either academically or athletically and embody the university spirit, ensuring honor and glory to the UVA legacy. While the Lawn Rooms don't actually have their own bathrooms or kitchens, residing on the Lawn is considered one of the university's greatest honors and not one you turn down for the sake of modern conveniences.

Behind the Pavilions and Lawn Rooms are ten gardens and, like the Pavilions, each garden is designed in a distinct way with no two gardens being the same. Together, the Rotunda, Lawn, Pavilions, and gardens make up the Academic Village that Jefferson designed and is today one of only six modern man-made UNESCO World Heritage Sites in the US. *Note: There are free student-led tours of the*

grounds offered daily throughout the year. Check out
www.visitcharlottesville.org *for more information.*

4. RUGBY ROAD AND THE CORNER

If you want a little slice of student life, look no further than **Rugby Road**, leading right into the heart of the Academic Village. Young men in khakis and navy blazers abound as the street is lined with IFC fraternity houses as well as other notable university buildings, such as The Fralin Museum of Art.

The Fralin Museum of Art is open to the public and is a great way to spend an hour, especially if you're an art aficionado. Occupying the historic Thomas H. Bayly building, its rotating exhibitions showcase hundreds of works, including African, Native American, and European American paintings, photography, and sculptures.

A stone's throw away from Rugby Road is the iconic **Corner** - a dazzling strand of boutique shops, clothing stores, bars, and eateries. While there is no actual corner, The Corner is best experienced on weekends after 6 pm when it becomes the hub of student nightlife. It is also one of the best places in town to go for a good meal. I recommend **Bodo's**, **Mellow Mushroom**, **Boylan Heights**, **Farm Bell Kitchen**, and **The Virginian** to name a few. And after a pub crawl, nothing satisfies that late-night boozy hunger like a cheesy Gus Burger (topped with a fried egg) at **The White Spot**!

On your walk to the Corner, you might pass by the **Memorial to Enslaved Laborers**. A stark reminder of the nation's troubled past, this monument pays tribute to the enslaved African American men and women who helped construct the beautiful buildings of Jefferson's Academic Village.

5. "GO HOOS!!" FOOTBALL AT SCOTT STADIUM

If you're a sports fan, then catching a UVA football game at Scott Stadium on a sunny fall afternoon should be at the top of your To-Do list. On game day, you can hear the roar of the crowd, the trumpeting of horns, and the "WAHOOWA" battle cry from miles away. Whether the Cavaliers are having a good year or not, the games are always well attended, and when the game is close, the seats literally shake with anticipation and excitement. However, this is not surprising when you consider that the stadium can pack in more than 60,000 Wahoos. Because of this, it is also used throughout the year to host other large events, such as concerts. Past acts include The Rolling Stones, U2, and Charlottesville's very own Dave Matthews Band.

6. BASKETBALL AT JPJ ARENA

Another must-do for sports fans is catching a basketball game at the John Paul Jones Arena (JPJ). This state-of-the-art facility was completed in 2006, replacing the much beloved U-Hall. However, the replacement was very necessary as it nearly doubled the seating capacity to accommodate over 14,000 fans. JPJ is now considered one of the biggest and best arenas in the ACC (Atlantic Coast Conference). Home to one of the top college basketball teams in the nation, the UVA men's team has a very impressive home court record of 206-46 as of March 2021. That being said, attending a men's or women's game at JPJ is not to be missed.

But just like Scott Stadium, sports aren't the only thing going on at JPJ. It too hosts a variety of other events throughout the year, such as Cirque du Soleil, The Wiggles, Disney on Ice, WWE Monday Night Raw, and many concerts. A wide range of groups have taken the stage at JPJ, including Metallica, Jay-Z, Bob Dylan, Taylor Swift, Phish, Bruce Springsteen, and Paul McCartney.

FOR THE HISTORY BUFFS

7. MONTICELLO

Here we are talking about Jefferson again, but this time, we'll take a look at his extravagant home and estate, Monticello (pronounced MON-tih-CHEL-oh); Italian for "little mountain."

Thomas Jefferson's Monticello

The beautiful home is 11,000 sq. feet and sits on 2,500 acres of land (about half of what it was originally). It has 33 different rooms (43 if you

23

include the attached Pavilions and South Terrace), showcasing some of Jefferson's most impressive inventions, and is considered his autobiographical masterpiece. It's even depicted on the reverse side of the US five-cent nickel!

Touring the home takes you back in time to the early days of a nascent country. Many tours are offered, both public and private, that walk you through the home and grounds, exploring private quarters as well as the West Lawn, the South Wing, and the iconic Dome Room. Guided tours double as history lessons, highlighting one of the nation's most important and influential figures as well as the complicated times in which he lived.

The land on which Monticello sits is a former plantation that produced tobacco, wheat, and various other crops. The gardens at Monticello were (and still are) a botanic marvel, best viewed during the spring or summer. They were also a source of food and an "experimental laboratory of ornamental and useful plants from around the world." Walking through the home and grounds is not only aesthetically pleasing but it's also a living, breathing history museum where a family can spend an entire day without ever noticing the time go by.

Despite Jefferson's vast accomplishments and role as a United States Founding Father, it is also necessary to note that his legacy does not come untarnished as he was a very prominent slave owner and most of his architectural achievements were built using slave labor. Monticello is committed to sharing an honest, inclusive history and offers many guided tours and exhibits that focus on the experiences of the enslaved people who lived and labored on the Monticello plantation. Nonetheless, the estate is still very culturally significant, and Monticello is included with the Rotunda and UVA grounds as a UNESCO World Heritage Site.

8. HIGHLAND

Highland, formerly known as Ash Lawn-Highland, was the home of James Monroe, the fifth president of the United States.

While the house itself is not nearly as impressive as neighboring Monticello, it is still very culturally and historically significant. It was only recently discovered within the past ten years that the main home was destroyed by a fire, most likely in 1829. The property today includes the 1818 guest house, an 1850s addition, and an 1870s Victorian Style farmhouse, along with various other reconstructed historic facilities.

Highland sits on a 535-acre working farm and is owned by Monroe's alma mater, the College of William & Mary. The property hosts over a dozen annual events, including the Albemarle County Fair and Historic Garden Week. The property also includes four miles of rustic trails that are free for public use.

9. MONTPELIER

If you're starting to get the impression that a lot of former US presidents lived in or around Charlottesville, you'd be right. Montpelier, located just outside of Charlottesville in neighboring Orange County, was home to James Madison, the fourth president of the United States. According to their website, the estate is "A memorial to James Madison and the Enslaved Community, a museum of American history, and a center for constitutional education that engages the public with the enduring legacy of Madison's most powerful idea: government by the people." (*Est. drive time: 40 minutes*)

Aside from simply touring the home, Montpelier also offers a plethora of hands-on learning activities throughout the year for both children and adults. The grounds include over eight miles of trails that meander through horse pastures, forests, and wildflower meadows while offering stunning views of the surrounding Blue Ridge Mountains. The estate also hosts a few annual events, most notably the Montpelier Hunt Races every fall, which is detailed in the "Fall Activities" section of this guide.

Again, it is important to note that all of the former presidential homes listed here were partially built and almost exclusively maintained by African American slave labor. Learning the complicated and disturbing truth about our nation's past is an important part of the overall experience when visiting these historical homes.

10. MICHIE TAVERN

After a morning spent touring a presidential home, you'll be hungry, and what better place to grab a bite than the historic Michie Tavern! Located a mere half mile from Monticello, this rustic restaurant takes you back to 1784, where servers adorned in period attire serve 18th-century southern classics, such as fried chicken, hickory-smoked pork barbeque, stewed tomatoes, black-eyed peas, green beans with country ham, and delicious buttermilk biscuits.

After filling your bellies, stroll over to the 1784 Pub for a post-meal beer or glass of wine in the oldest section of Michie Tavern. Or you can peruse their various shops, all housed in distinct historic structures. Please note that the restaurant is currently only open for lunch. However, Michie Tavern does host private group dinners to create a unique and memorable experience, perfect for wedding rehearsals and receptions, corporate events, or various other special occasions

GET OUTSIDE!

Charlottesville is by all definitions a four-season city. Every season has a distinct feel and vibe to it, as well as an abundance of outdoor activities that are complemented by the seasonal weather. Here are the top six activities to experience in C-ville depending on the time of year you visit.

SUMMER ACTIVITIES

11. KAYAKING, CANOEING, OR TUBING DOWN THE RIVANNA RIVER

Beginning in the spring and continuing through the summer into fall, this activity is a local favorite. The Rivanna River Co. offers a variety of different kayaking and canoeing options, with trips ranging from an easy one-hour paddle to more exciting and challenging 3–4-hour trips through Class I & II rapids.

31

If paddling isn't your thing, then plop into an inflated tube and let the gentle flow of the river do all the work. Whatever option you choose, the route is lined with sandy beaches, perfect for picnics, and swimming holes, perfect for... swimming! *Note: Another great option for the same activity is James River Reeling and Rafting located just outside of the city in Scottsville.*

12. THE SHENANDOAH NATIONAL PARK

The Shenandoah National Park (SNP) is Charlottesville's - indeed Virginia's - premier outdoor playground with more than 200,000 acres of protected land. Activities are plentiful and include hiking, biking, camping, picnicking, leaf peeping, ranger programs, and wildlife spotting. Speaking of wildlife, the park is home to a wide range of animals, including deer, bobcats, dozens of species of birds and reptiles, and, most exciting of all, black bears. There are also visitor centers and "waysides" open during the summer, offering snacks, burgers, and blackberry milkshakes (highly recommended). (*Est. drive time to south entrance: 40 min.*)

While there are activities for every season here, summertime is best for hiking and camping. There are hundreds of miles of hiking trails, including 101 miles of the iconic Appalachian Trail that runs from Springer Mountain in Georgia to Katahdin in Maine. An average hike in the park might pass by cascading waterfalls, refreshing swim holes, breathtaking vistas, fields of wildflowers, serene wooded hollows, or all of the above! *Note: there is a National Park fee per vehicle required upon entry.*

If you have the time and inclination, I recommend an overnight camping trip. There are dozens of three-walled shelters that are free to use, as well as designated campgrounds and picnic areas. You might even encounter an AT thru-hiker; a person who is hiking the entire Appalachian Trail (roughly 2,189 miles) in one hiking season. You can always tell a thru-hiker by their rugged look, chiseled legs, and their exceptional smell! If you cross paths with an AT thru-hiker in the wild, feel free to ask them questions about their journey and always offer them candy or snacks if you have any to spare (they're perpetually hungry). On the other hand, if you encounter a black bear, stay calm, keep your distance, and never under any circumstances try to feed them. Pictures of a black bear in the wild are great; having an unpleasant experience with a black bear because you tempted it with food is definitely NOT great.

13. FISHING AND SWIMMING AT A PUBLIC LAKE

Several lakes around Charlottesville are open to the public and provide a great place to go fishing and swimming.

Whether the fish population is stocked or self-sustained, you're bound to catch something. Most of the lakes offer a fishing pier or platform, and some have canoes available for rental. Expect to reel in bass, catfish, panfish, and the occasional trout. *Note: make sure to check if a fishing permit is needed before you go, and most lakes charge a small fee for entry.*

If you get tired of fishing, lay out on a sandy beach or go for a swim! Most of the lakes have grills and picnic areas set up, and some even have concession stands that are open during the summer months. There are usually a few hiking trails nearby as well. The most popular lakes to visit would be Chris Greene Lake, Walnut Creek, and Mint Springs.

14. PUBLIC POOLS

Ok, so maybe you'd rather swim where the water is clear and you can see your feet. Not a problem! There are three public pools and four spray grounds (for children) that are guaranteed to keep visitors cool during the heat of summer. Washington Park Pool, Onesty Family Aquatic Center, and Smith Aquatic & Fitness Center are available to both residents and non-residents for nominal fees. They even include waterslides, diving areas, and specific sections for swimming laps.

15. POLO MATCHES

If you're looking for a unique and fun way to spend a Sunday afternoon, you've found it. Roseland Polo matches at King Family Vineyard are scheduled every Sunday at noon, from Memorial Day through October, weather permitting. The matches are completely free and open to the public with no reservation required. Tailgating is permitted starting at 10 am and there is a selection of food trucks available on-site. Of course, premium wine is also available before, during, and after the match. After all, it *is* at a vineyard!

Polo matches are a great way to spend a Sunday afternoon.

16. THE SKATE PARK

Skate or die! The Charlottesville Skate Park offers some of the best street and vert skating facilities in the state. There is the street plaza section with rails, ramps, and ledges, and then there's the vert area with concrete pools and half pipes.

While skateboarding is the main sport here, bikes, scooters, and rollerblades are also welcome. However, be advised that the skate park is an unsupervised facility and all participants assume complete responsibility for accidents and injuries.

FALL ACTIVITIES

17. APPLE PICKING ON CARTER MOUNTAIN

Literally down the road from Monticello is Carter Mountain Orchard - the perfect place to spend an autumn afternoon picking delicious, crisp apples. The orchard is open year-round but it's best to visit in the fall. The views from atop the mountain are spectacular and once the fall foliage starts to kick in, they can't be beat. Fall Festivities include pumpkin picking and hayrides around the orchard. And if you go on a Thursday, the mountain is hopping with live music, food, and hard cider while the sun sets as part of their Thursday Evening Sunset Series.

The Country Store & Bakery offers every kind of apple product you can imagine along with other fruit treats. There's even a brewery on-site, Bold Rock Tap Room, that offers a selection of craft hard ciders and seltzers. By the time you leave, you'll have a trunk full of hand-picked apples, fresh-pressed apple cider, apple cider donuts (highly addictive), and homemade apple pie.

18. LEAF PEEPING ON THE SKYLINE DRIVE

Yes, leaf peeping is a real thing and as I mentioned before, the fall foliage in Virginia is incredible. But when viewed from one of the lookout points along the Skyline Drive, it simply takes your breath away.

Fall is the best time to go leaf peeping on the Skyline Drive

The Skyline Drive is a public road that runs 105 miles along the crest of the Blue Ridge Mountains. Originally built in the 1930s as the main feature of what was to become the Shenandoah National Park, it is now a National Scenic Byway as well as a National Historic Landmark. There are dozens of sweeping overlooks (75 to be exact) along the drive where one can stop and look out over seemingly endless miles of valley below. During late fall, it's as if you're gazing upon an undulating sea of red, orange, and gold. (*Est. drive time to the southern terminus: 40 min.*)

US Senator Harry F. Byrd of Virginia once said of the Skyline Drive, "It is a wonder way over which the tourist will ride comfortably in his car while he is stirred by a view as exhilarating as the aviator may see from the plane." Over 80 years later, nothing has changed. *Note: the fee for entering SNP is required upon entry.*

19. EPIC AUTUMN HIKES

Hiking during the fall in Virginia is a must. There are literally hundreds of day hikes in and around Charlottesville if you include what the Shenandoah National Park has to offer. However, two hikes in particular come to mind when I think of the ultimate views for fall foliage leaf peepers. Those are Humpback Rock and Old Rag Mountain.

Humpback Rock is located just south of SNP and therefore does not require a fee for entry. There is a four-mile trail loop that leads straight up to the summit and then gradually back down via the Appalachian Trail. The trail up is well-maintained but has an elevation gain of 740 feet so be prepared to break a sweat. However, the views from the peak are well worth the effort. The massive rocky outcropping offers a 360-degree view of the surrounding mountains and valleys; uber-Instagrammable during the fall. (*Est. drive time to trailhead: 45 min.*)

Old Rag Mountain is part of SNP and therefore requires the fee. It is also possibly the most popular day-hike in the park so don't expect to have the summit to yourself. However, there is plenty of space to spread out on this grand rocky summit. The trail up is much more difficult and longer (9-mile circuit or 5.4-mile up and back) than the Humpback Rock trail and is not recommended for beginner hikers or young children. I would suggest making a day trip out of Old Rag Mountain by combining it with a ride along the Skyline Drive. *Note: due to the hike's popularity, a day-hike ticket might be required for this hike. (Est. drive time to trailhead: 1 hr. 45 min.)*

If hiking up mountains doesn't suit your fancy, there are plenty of local nature areas within the Charlottesville city limits. Sure, they may not offer the views, but you'll be surrounded by nature and beautiful foliage just the same. I'd recommend **Ivy Creek Natural Area**, with more than seven miles of walking trails through serene forests and diverse habitats. The trails are maintained by the Ivy Creek Foundation and make for a perfect leisurely stroll, including a paved trail for visitors with mobility impairments. While you're there, make sure you check out the barn, which was part of the River View Farm. River View Farm was established by former slave Hugh Carr shortly after emancipation and is now an integral part of African American Heritage in Virginia.

20. WINE TASTING AND VINEYARD TOURS

Virginia very well might be the Wine Country of the East Coast, with more than 30 wineries and vineyards in the Charlottesville area alone. Whether you're new to wine or have enjoyed it for years, C-ville wines offer something for every palate.

Most wine enthusiasts will tell you that wine tours are best after summer. Tasting rooms are usually less crowded in the fall, meaning you'll get more attention, plus the temperature is cooler, which makes for a more enjoyable amble through the vineyards. C-ville is home to large vineyards that have been producing wine for several decades as well as smaller, family-owned vineyards where you'll find a cozier tasting experience. **The Monticello Wine Trail** includes 30+ wineries of all shapes and sizes, each with its own unique personality and atmosphere. Many wineries have stunning mountain views and are great spots to admire the landscape. You can even stay on-site at several wineries in the area for the ultimate vineyard vacation!

21. THE MONTPELIER HUNT RACES

There's an old saying in Orange County that goes, "You might miss Christmas, but you won't miss the races." The sentiment still holds true today. This event, always held on the first Saturday in November, began in 1934 on the front lawn of James Madison's home. It is now one of the premier horse races of the National Steeplechase Association circuit and features the only live brush jumps in Virginia. *(Est. drive time: 40 min.)*

However, this event isn't just about horses. The day begins with a crowd favorite, the Terrier Races, where dogs compete over hurdles for the award of "Most Prestigious Pup!" Following that is the exceedingly adorable children's Stick Horse Race. The main event begins shortly after noon and wraps up by 5 p.m. There are also other events, such as the hat contest and the vintage car display. And, as with any horse race, lavish tailgating is ubiquitous. However, you won't find the event as chaotic as the Foxfield races in spring, where UVA students turn the race day into an all-out booze fest.

While you're in the area, make sure to check out some of the local wineries, the traditional Village of Gordonsville, or the Liberty Mill Farm, home to the country's largest corn maze!

22. TRICK-OR-TREATING ON THE LAWN

If you happen to be in C-ville on Halloween, don your spookiest costume and go trick-or-treating on UVA's Lawn.

A longtime tradition established by students in the late 80s, Trick-or-Treating on the Lawn is a highly anticipated event for students, children, and parents alike. The turnout is usually colossal, making it a fun and safe way to celebrate Halloween. Lawn residents and members of student organizations are stationed in each of the 54 Lawn Rooms to give out treats and candy. Talk about a massive haul, your sweet tooth will be satisfied until Christmas!

WINTER ACTIVITIES

23. SKIING/SNOWBOARDING AT WINTERGREEN

Wintergreen Resort offers the best slopes for skiing and snowboarding near Charlottesville. Boasting 26 slopes and trails, there's terrain for newbies to advanced skiers and riders. The resort also has lit areas for night skiing, a terrain park with over 40 features to accommodate a variety of skill levels, and The Plunge - Virginia's largest tubing park. If you're into winter sports, this is the place to be. *(Est. drive time: 1 hr.)*

Skiing and snowboarding is fun for the entire family!

Is it a mild winter in Virginia? Don't fret, Wintergreen is home to one of the world's most sophisticated snowmaking systems, SNOWPOWER. According to their website, "Theoretically with optimal conditions, Wintergreen Resort's snowmaking system could cover a football field with 37 feet of snow in just 24 hours." Now that's a manmade blizzard of epic proportions!

24. MASSANUTTEN

Massanutten is also a popular destination for central Virginia skiers and snowboarders. However, with only 16 runs for varying skill levels, the riding options are decidedly less at Massanutten when compared to Wintergreen. Nonetheless, it also has a tubing park, a terrain park, and lit areas for night skiing. *(Est. drive time: 1 hr.)*

But there is one big draw that Massanutten has over Wintergreen, and that is an indoor waterpark! With temperatures set at 84 degrees year-round, you can hit the slopes all morning and then spend the afternoon relaxing your aching muscles on the lazy river until it's time for dinner. The indoor portion of the Massanutten Waterpark includes a veritable water fortress, inflatable rides, body slides, pools, hot tubs, and surfing on the FlowRider Endless Wave. Once summertime rolls around, the waterpark doubles in size with an outdoor portion. Together, Massanutten's Waterpark is one of the best in the country.

25. LIGHTING OF THE LAWN

Let there be light! As the holiday season rolls around, there are various "lightings" throughout C-ville to get people in the holiday mood. Two of the best lightings would be the Lighting of the Lawn and Charlottesville's Grand Illumination.

The Lighting of the Lawn began in the wake of the 9/11 attacks to foster unity and inclusion in the UVA and Charlottesville communities. It immediately became an annual event, occurring every year around the first week of December on UVA's Lawn. This momentous celebration invites thousands of attendees to gather in front of the Rotunda and watch as it, along with the Pavilions and Lawn Rooms, are lit up with a dazzling array of lights and colors from every corner of the spectrum. The event has an extremely joyful, if not party, vibe to it as performances from student acapella groups fill the brisk night air with harmonized music and cheer.

26. CHARLOTTESVILLE'S GRAND ILLUMINATION

Also occurring during the first week of December and equally as momentous is Charlottesville's Grand Illumination. This spectacular tree lighting event features music, food, games, prizes, special guests (specifically a jolly old man in red and his favorite reindeer), and holiday fun for all ages.

The event is held on the east end of the Downtown Mall, near the Ting Pavilion. The festivities usually kick off around 5 pm, with acclaimed musical acts from all over the county playing at the Pavilion. There's a children's Winter Wonderland area with bounce houses, face painting, games, special guests, and rides aboard the Holiday Train. For adults, there are dozens of Holiday Market vendors serving up hot food and beverages, including a great selection of craft beers and wine. After the sun sets and nighttime arrives, the Pavilion is lit up with stunning projections, and the event's finale, a countdown to the Grand Illumination of the Holiday Tree with over 20,000 LED lights, transforms the City Hall Plaza into a glowing holiday spectacle.

27. THE HOLIDAY MARKET

An extension of the weekly City Market (see the "Shop 'til you Drop" section), the Holiday Market is held every Saturday in December leading up to Christmas and offers a variety of unique gifts, decorations, food, and crafts made by local farmers, artists, and bakers. What better place to find a special gift for that one family member or friend who is impossible to shop for!

28. FIRST NIGHT VIRGINIA

Every year begins on a good note when you spend your New Year's Eve at First Night Virginia. Families and visitors are treated to a plethora of entertainment acts in and around the Downtown Mall, such as live music, magic performances, laser light shows, and a fantastic fireworks spectacle to celebrate the New Year. C-ville even has its very own ball drop at the stroke of midnight. This is a family-friendly event that you'll definitely allow the kiddies to stay up for.

SPRING ACTIVITIES

29. THE RIVANNA TRAILS

Once springtime rolls around and warmer weather makes its way into central Virginia, people are itching to get outside. Fortunately, C-ville has the perfect setup for a walk or bike ride around the city via the Rivanna Trails.

The Rivanna Trails circuit consists of over 20 miles of well-maintained trails, pathways, and greenways that are connected to circumnavigate the entire city. This provides locals and visitors with a great opportunity to get outside and exercise, as well as explore the city by foot or bike. It's especially pleasant during the springtime as flowers begin to bloom, and blossoming trees extend their canopies with bright leaves and lush greenery.

30. HOT AIR BALLOON RIDES

Probably the best and most unique way to view the blossoming splendor of the Blue Ridge Mountains is by floating thousands of feet above ground in a hot air balloon.

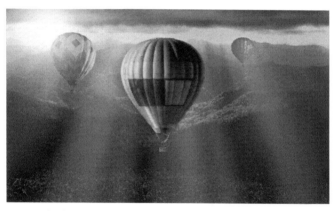

Watch the sun rise or set over the mountains while floating in a hot air balloon.

There are a couple of different companies that offer balloon trips, one being the family-owned and operated Blue Ridge Ballooning. Their launch site is five minutes from downtown and they offer a wide range of packages, including sunrise and sunset flights which culminate in a champagne celebration. This is truly a once-in-a-lifetime adventure and a memory that you will cherish for years to come. *Note: all flights are weather permitting and children under 7 years old are not recommended for this activity.*

31. GOLF

Ok, so maybe you'd prefer to keep your feet on the ground. In that case, how about a round of golf? With natural fairways over rolling hills, and course trails that meander along running streams shaded by graceful willows and ancient oaks, golfing in C-ville is the perfect springtime activity, whether you're a novice or an expert.

There are four courses in the immediate area, including fairways with 4 ½-star rankings from Golf Digest, links designed by Pete Dye, and an Arnold Palmer Signature Course. Look up Birdwood, Meadowcreek, Old Trail, or Lake Monticello golf courses to inquire about tee times and rates.

32. HISTORIC GARDEN WEEK

For one week in April, visitors can tour private landscapes, public gardens, and historic sites across Albemarle County, enjoying the exquisite beauty of the area during the peak of spring. In addition, world-class floral arrangements created by the Garden Club of Virginia will enhance tour properties.

The beginning of Historic Garden Week dates back to 1927 when a flower show organized by the Garden Club of Virginia raised an impressive $7,000 to save trees planted by Thomas Jefferson on the lawn at Monticello. Almost 100 years later, it has become a highly anticipated statewide event consisting of 30+ unique tours organized and hosted by 48 member clubs located from the foothills of the Shenandoah Valley to the beaches of Tidewater. The participating properties in and around C-ville include all the historic presidential homes as well as the Pavilion gardens on the UVA grounds.

33. THE DOGWOOD FESTIVAL

April is a busy month for C-ville when it seems as though every weekend has its own bustling itinerary. This is especially so during the annual Dogwood Festival; a weeklong event that hosts a slew of family-friendly activities, including the Dogwood Track Classic, Pageant, Queen's Ball, Home Run Derby, Benefit Breakfast, and the Dogwood Eggstravaganza.

The centerpiece attraction is the Dogwood Grand Parade, which makes its way down Main Street and through the Downtown Mall. The parade features dazzling floats, C-ville celebrities, mascots, true-life heroes, high school marching bands, and the Dogwood Court Princesses. The event is rounded out with another fantastic fireworks display at night.

There's also the Dogwood Carnival, featuring a variety of classic to thrilling rides for both children and adults. The Carnival is set up at the beginning of the festival and usually stays on for an additional week after the festival ends.

34. FOXFIELD RACES

The Foxfield Races are part of the steeplechase circuit and are held bi-annually in the spring and fall. However, it is the springtime race, which attracts more than 20,000 attendees, that you want to go to.

The springtime Foxfield Races have become a tradition of sorts for UVA students, as well as students from neighboring universities. The day usually begins somewhat tame and graceful, with everyone in attendance decked out in their Sunday's best and grazing on extravagant spreads while sipping high-end wines and spirits. As the day progresses, however, revelry ensues and by the end of the event, you may feel as though you're wandering through an open-field frat party. Many students go simply for that reason - to enjoy the tailgate party - and leave while proudly boasting that they "never saw a horse!" *Note: the event's organizers are working to curb the out-of-control drinking so as to keep the event classy, as it was originally intended to be.*

Regardless of the party aspect, the Foxfield races are still a lot of fun and can be enjoyed by the entire family.

SHOP 'TIL YOU DROP

35. THE DOWNTOWN MALL

A visit to C-ville isn't complete without spending a day at the city's vibrant core, the Downtown Mall. One of the longest pedestrian walking malls in the US, it is a bustling agora of restaurants, bars, cafes, and dozens of boutique shops housed in a hip mix of renovated and restored historic buildings. However, you won't find any retail stores or brand name outlets here. The best thing about shopping on the downtown mall is that almost all the shops are locally owned and operated, offering a wide range of specialty products, gifts, and apparel.

Once you've finished your shopping spree, choose from a plethora of al fresco dining options for a delicious meal. After your meal, catch a movie, play, or concert at one of the several performance venues, including the historic Paramount Theater and Jefferson Theater (see the "Entertainment & Nightlife" section of this guide for more information on the theaters). And still, there's more to do with a nightlife that is nearly unmatched except for the

Corner. There's even a free trolley service that connects the Downtown Mall to the UVA grounds making it easy for visitors to get around. With so much to do, you can see how it's easy to spend a full day at the Downtown Mall alone.

36. BARRACKS ROAD

Barracks Road Shopping Center is where most of the locals go to shop as it brings together the best of local and national brands in one convenient spot just minutes away from UVA. Here, retail giants such as Barnes & Noble and Bed Bath & Beyond stand hand in hand with specialty boutiques, such as The Virginia Shop and Great Outdoor Provision Co. There are also plenty of coffee shops and familiar eateries to keep you energized, such as Starbucks, Five Guys Burgers, and Panera Bread.

37. THE SHOPS AT STONEFIELD

Another excellent shopping option is The Shops at Stonefield. Designed as a unique gathering place for the local community, it features outdoor dining, pocket parks, and a central plaza. A pedestrian-friendly environment links best-in-class retail with a variety of dining and entertainment experiences. Speaking of entertainment, there is a 65,000-square-foot Regal ScreenX & IMAX movie theater with 14 screens. This newer addition to the C-ville shopping scene is a center specifically created as a natural extension of the area's historic aesthetics and one-of-a-kind culture.

38. CITY MARKETS

These are the ultimate farmer's markets, located minutes away from the Downtown Mall and open every Saturday, April through December, from 8 am till noon. There are actually two separate markets, the first one situated on the corner of Second and Market Street, adjacent to the Downtown Mall. The second one is located at IX Art Park, less than half a mile away. At these markets, you'll find everything from seasonal fruits and veggies to handmade gifts, jewelry, and fresh baked goods. The markets feature over 100 vendors during peak season and are a great way to spend your Saturday morning. Don't forget to grab a cup of artisan coffee to go with your fresh-out-the-fryer spudnuts!

WHO'S HUNGRY?

39. BODO'S BAGELS

I'm not exaggerating when I say that this is probably the best bagel shop in the world. Seriously, I've had bagels from Jewish bakeries in New York and they still don't compare. And I'm not alone in my assessment - it's been voted "Best Sandwich" in *Cville Weekly* for going on 30 years!

This place has bagel production down to a science. Crisp on the outside, soft and doughy on the inside, the bagels practically melt in your mouth. They're open early in the morning for breakfast and remain busy through lunch and dinner, until they close at 8 pm. I personally recommend the deli egg on everything with Swiss cheese, lettuce, tomato, onion, easy mayo, cut, with a pickle slice on the side.

However, bagels aren't the only thing they serve. They also have hearty soups and delicious green salads, as well as potato salad and tabouli salad.

Everything they serve is made on-site and the bagels are constantly being baked throughout the day, so "stale" does not exist in this establishment. Best of all, it's very affordable (I would say "cheap" but I don't want to undermine the quality), and no matter how busy they get, the service is always pretty quick. There are three locations: one on Preston Avenue near downtown, one on Emmet Street near Barracks Road, and one on the Corner at UVA. The Emmet Street location even offers soft-serve ice cream for dessert!

40. RIVERSIDE

This place is a classic. Serving up burgers and hot dogs since 1935, this is one of C-ville's favorite greasy spoons. However, it's the burgers that people come for. Just looking at them, they're not all that impressive, but there's something about these flat-pressed burgers that's just so darn good that you might find yourself eating two or even three in a sitting! The place is laid-back and always full of locals.

41. DAIRY MARKET

Not sure what you're in the mood for? Then head over to the Dairy Market - a modern-day food hall housed in the revamped Monticello Dairy building that dates back to 1937!

"A carnivore and a vegan walk into a (Dairy) Market..." sounds like the beginning of an offbeat joke but here, it's a regular occurrence. Currently, the Market is made up of 17 merchants: 12 food merchants, a brewery, one full-service restaurant, one bar, and two retail stalls. The food options here are truly international; from the zesty Thai-inspired Chimm St. to the Latin American street food of Maizal, to the authentic Filipino dishes found at Manila Street, there is undoubtedly something for everyone. Wash it all down with a curated cocktail from The Milkman's Bar or a local craft brew from Starr Hill Brewery. For dessert, trace it all back to the building's roots with a stop by Moo Thru, offering "real ice cream from real dairy farmers."

It's not all about the food, though. You might find yourself shopping for clothes, home goods, or a variety of specialty products while you're there. Plus, they host pop-up events and live music all throughout the year so there's always something going on. It's also worth mentioning that the space is tailored to promote Virginia farm-to-table restaurants while encouraging a diverse market and offering minority entrepreneurs a space of their own, with 22% of the vendors being women-owned and 33% minority-owned.

42. HAMILTONS' AT FIRST & MAIN

Located on the Downtown Mall, Hamiltons' is the perfect spot for a delicious afternoon lunch on their outdoor patio or a fancy romantic dinner in their fine dining interior.

Offering contemporary gourmet American cuisine, the rotating menu features locally sourced vegetables, fresh meats, seafood, and a vegetarian "blue plate special." The intimate atmosphere and attentive service ensure that their guests enjoy an outstanding dining experience, be they C-ville natives, visitors, or UVA students and alumni. As many restaurants come and go on the Downtown Mall, Hamiltons' has stood the test of time as a local favorite for decades.

43. IVY INN

This exquisite local gem is located in a house that dates back to the early 19th century and is less than a mile away from the UVA grounds. The menu features delicious locally-inspired American cuisine with a decidedly southern flare. The atmosphere is rustic, with a simple yet elegant indoor dining area as well as an outdoor patio to enjoy the beautiful central Virginia weather. That being said, reservations are highly encouraged as this restaurant stays busy all throughout the year.

WHERE TO STAY

44. KESWICK HALL

If you're looking for luxury in C-ville, you'll find it in this sprawling property just seven miles outside of the city center. Brimming with amenities, this place exudes opulence and indulgence.

Since 1912, Keswick Hall has been known for elegance, grandeur, and a sense of true peace within the Virginia hills. The luxury hotel suites come complete with mountain vista views, and with so many pampering opportunities, you may find it hard to leave the premises. You can spend your entire trip taking in the alluring landscape from the infinity-edge Horizon Pool, getting massages and holistic treatment at the spa, teeing off on the 18-hole Pete Dye-designed golf course, or simply sipping handcrafted cocktails by the pool. And once you've worked up an appetite, you'll be treated to an unforgettable dining experience provided by Michelin-starred chef Jean-Georges Vongerichten

45. BOAR'S HEAD RESORT

Boar's Head is a quintessential Virginia resort, offering a warm, intimate ambiance, exceptional service, and unparalleled southern hospitality.

Located on a 600-acre estate, a stay at Boar's Head invites guests to explore their network of nature trails, play a round of golf on their championship course, or enjoy their world-class fitness club and aquatics facility. You can renew your body and soul at their spa before savoring the fare at their legendary Mill Room. And if all of that isn't enough to do, Boar's Head hosts family-friendly events year-round, including their Summer Celebration Series and Winter Wander. Much like C-ville, this four-diamond country resort blends the best with the best - classic with contemporary, refined with casual, tranquil with dynamic.

46. OAKHURST INN

Focusing a little less on luxury and more on history and simple elegance is the delightful Oakhurst Inn. Nestled in one of C-ville's most prestigious neighborhoods and mere steps away from the University grounds, the Oakhurst Inn brings charming accommodations, creative cuisine, and a welcoming space where visitors and locals can connect.

Formerly three boarding houses and the home of a university professor, the Craftsman-era residences that makeup Oakhurst Inn date back to 1913. 100 years later, careful renovations were made focused on preserving the unique architectural features of the homes while incorporating modern design elements and amenities. It reopened in 2014 as a boutique inn, offering 36 quaint guest rooms, the Chateau Lobby Bar, the Oakhurst Inn Cafe, a saltwater pool and deck, and complimentary valet parking. Adjacent to the UVA hospital and grounds, the location couldn't be more central to everything that C-ville offers. And with the subtle elegance and grace of the accommodations, you'll feel as though you never left home.

47. THE CLIFTON

Rustic and country elegance are the words I'd use to describe this boutique hotel set on 100 acres of central Virginia countryside. Here is yet another unique opportunity to stay in a comfortable home steeped in history.

The historic inns that make up The Clifton were originally constructed in 1799 as a classic colonial-style home for Thomas Jefferson's daughter and husband, Martha and Thomas Mann Randolph. In the spring of 2018, the award-winning Blackberry Farm Design team came in to reimagine the Inn's interiors with both an appreciation for past style and an eye toward the future. The result is a chic contemporary take on a classic country estate - a dramatic yet romantic destination for families, couples, weddings, and meetings steeped in the heritage and beauty of the area.

Incorporating mid-century details throughout all of its spaces, The Clifton includes 20 guest rooms spanning five late 18th and early 19th century buildings, a restaurant, bar and lounge, and a wine cellar. Updated amenities include an infinity pool and hot tub while property features include a private lake, walking trails, a croquet lawn, and sprawling gardens with a special Chef's Garden for the restaurant. Speaking of restaurants, the 1799 Restaurant is one of the best in the area and the seasonal menu showcases food that is distinctive to the Mid-Atlantic region. The cuisine is perfectly paired with an extensive wine selection featuring Virginia's most celebrated wines along with vintages from around the world.

ENTERTAINMENT & NIGHTLIFE

48. FRIDAYS AFTER FIVE & THE TING PAVILION

Fridays After Five on the Downtown Mall has been a C-ville tradition for decades. From April to September, this free concert series is always the best way to relax and unwind after a busy week at work.

The music is played on the east end of the Downtown Mall at the city's premier outdoor music venue, the Ting Pavilion. You can expect a wide range of local music, from bluegrass to R&B to the immortal songs of The Beatles played by C-ville's Abbey Road. While you listen, multiple vendors are selling local microbrews, wines, and ciders to help you let go of work and welcome the weekend. There are also food trucks aplenty to keep your stomach from growling.

The Ting Pavilion also hosts big-name musical acts all year long. Bands such as The Avett Brothers,

Sheryl Crow, The Flaming Lips, Joan Baez & Indigo Girls, Alison Krauss, Beck, Snoop Dogg, Willie Nelson, Vampire Weekend, and The Beach Boys have all graced the stage at the Pavilion along with hundreds of others. If you take into account JPJ, Scott Stadium, and the dozens of smaller venues throughout town, it is easy to deduce that C-ville is one of the best cities in the country for live music.

49. BREWERIES AND THE CHARLOTTESVILLE ALE TRAIL

As micro-breweries have become ubiquitous in cities throughout the nation, nowhere is that more apparent than C-ville. One might say that it started with Starr Hill Brewery in 1999, which has become one of the most awarded craft breweries on the East Coast. Now the city boasts more than a dozen breweries (not counting the 30+ wineries) offering the full gamut of lagers, ales, stouts, and ciders. A few worth mentioning are Starr Hill, South Street, Rockfish, and Three Notch'd breweries.

You could spend a week partying in C-ville and not get through all the craft beers and ciders that are local to the area. That is, not until the **Charlottesville Ale Trail** came along to assist you on your libation quest! As the premier urban beer trail in Virginia, the objective of the Ale Trail is to promote the vibrant craft-brewing industry within walking distance of the downtown area. Every point on the trail is within a reasonable walking distance of each other, totaling 1.5 miles. There's even a digital passport program where trail goers can visit each brewery on the trail and claim a stamp. Collect all the stamps and submit your passport for a prize. Imagine that - a prize for drinking! Hopefully you'll still be able to walk by the time you finish the trail!

50. THE DOWNTOWN MALL (JEFFERSON AND PARAMOUNT THEATERS)

A place so nice, I had to mention it twice! However, this time I'm focusing on the spirited nightlife on the mall. If you're looking to get loose on a Friday or Saturday (or even a Monday), head downtown for a bar-hopping experience you won't forget - if only you could remember it! From the long-standing Miller's to the hip Livery Stable to the cozy Whiskey Jar, the Downtown Mall has so many options for drinking and fun that it will make your head spin! Or is that just the tequila talking?

There are also two theaters worth mentioning, both equally historic and iconic: the Jefferson Theater and the Paramount Theater.

The **Jefferson Theater** was established in 1912 as a live performance theater that played host to silent movies, vaudeville acts, and a historic list of live performers, ranging from Harry Houdini to The Three Stooges. After a comprehensive restoration that kept the theater's vintage architecture while modernizing its facilities, the Jefferson reopened in 2009 with two full-service bars, a restored balcony, and a state-of-the-art sound and lighting system, making it a truly awesome venue for live music. It has a steady roster of bands performing throughout the week, year-round.

The **Paramount Theater** opened its doors in 1931 as one of the last grand "movie palaces" during the golden age of cinema. Designed by the Chicago architectural firm of Rapp & Rapp, the Paramount boasts a stately Georgian facade, elegant lobby, magnificent chandeliers, exquisite plaster moldings, and an ornate auditorium. It closed in 1974 but reopened 30 years later following a decade of fundraising and two years of renovation and expansion. With a mission to "educate, enchant, enrich, and enlighten through the power of the arts," it now hosts nationally acclaimed performances, classic movies, speakers, special screenings, and a diverse menu of live events each year.

51. VIRGINIA THEATRE FESTIVAL

UVA's Department of Drama believes that theatre is a vital form of artistic expression in today's world, presenting theatre and dance performances throughout the year. Their state-of-the-art venues include the 520-seat Culbreth Theatre with a proscenium stage, the flexible 160-200-seat Helms Theatre, and the 300-seat Ruth Caplin Theatre with a thrust stage.

Since 1974, UVA has hosted the Virginia Theatre Festival every summer, treating students and community members far and wide to a summer line-up of well-rounded, professional productions. Leading directors, designers, technicians, and actors from across the country form the company each year to produce a season of Broadway musicals, classic works, and contemporary plays.

BONUS TIPS: DAY TRIPS

52. RICHMOND

Richmond is Virginia's capital and is located only an hour east of C-ville. This makes it a quick and easy day trip for anyone looking for a change of scenery.

As the state capital, Richmond is home to many of Virginia's finest museums, including the Virginia Museum of Fine Arts, the Science Museum of Virginia, and the Virginia Museum of History and Culture. Like C-ville, Richmond is also very historically significant. St. John's Episcopal Church - the site of Patrick Henry's famous "Give me liberty or give me death" speech - still stands today and is a popular place to visit, as well as the Richmond National Battlefield Park and the American Civil War Center at Historic Tredegar Iron Works (Richmond was the capital of the Confederacy during the Civil War). The Edgar Allen Poe Museum, featuring many of his writings and artifacts from his life, makes for a good visit, as does the somber yet important Richmond Slave Trail.

Other places of interest include Maymont; a 100-acre Victorian estate and public park, which features the Maymont Mansion, an arboretum, formal gardens, a carriage collection, a nature center, and a children's farm. Belle Isle, a 54-acre island that lies in the middle of the James River, is also worth checking out. There, visitors can stroll the nature trails, go swimming, rock-climbing, or birdwatching, or simply take in the sweeping skyline views. And if you're into racing, then the Richmond Raceway is a must. Known as America's Premier Short Track, the raceway hosts the NASCAR Cup Series, NASCAR Xfinity Series, and the NASCAR Camping World Truck Series.

Richmond also offers great shopping, excellent restaurants, and a vibrant live music and art scene. I'd recommend spending an afternoon shopping the indie boutiques and vintage emporiums in the bohemian district of Carytown before stopping by Garnett's for one of their famous sandwiches and a pint of local craft beer. Top the night off with live music by Richmond's own Carbon Leaf at The National Theater on Broad Street.

53. WASHINGTON D.C.

A two-and-a-half-hour drive north of C-ville will bring you to the US capitol, Washington D.C. This city needs no explanation; the title says it all. I will, however, mention a few must-see sites and activities.

The US Capitol building

The obvious sites to see include the Washington Monument and Lincoln Memorial, as well as the iconic buildings that house the federal government's three branches: the Capitol, White House, and Supreme Court. The National Mall, located between the Lincoln Memorial and the Capitol, is a large open park that hosts many events, including presidential inaugurations, concerts, and festivals. It has also been the site of numerous political protests throughout the years. The National Mall is surrounded by multiple memorials, including one for every war the US has ever been a part of, and about a dozen museums.

As far as museums go, you could spend weeks exploring them all and still not see everything there is to see. Most of the museums are part of the Smithsonian Institution - the largest research and museum complex in the world. The best part about the Smithsonian museums, which include the National Zoo, is that they're free of charge! If you only have a few days, I'd recommend one or two of the following: the National Museum of Natural History, the National Air and Space Museum, the National Museum of American History, the National Museum of the American Indian, the National Gallery of Art, or the United States Holocaust Memorial Museum.

Washington D.C. is also the national center for the arts. The iconic Kennedy Center is home to the National Symphony Orchestra, the Washington National Opera, and the Washington Ballet. The historic Ford's Theatre, where Lincoln was assassinated, continues to operate as a performance space as well as a museum. A thriving performing arts scene includes a handful of nationally respected professional companies, such as the Shakespeare Theatre Company, Arena Stage, Woolly Mammoth Theatre Company, and Studio Theatre. Also, the country's oldest professional musical organization, the United States Marine Band is housed at the Marine Barracks near Capitol Hill.

When it comes to sports, take your pick. No matter what sport you're into, Washington has a professional team. For football, you have the Washington Commanders (formerly the Washington Redskins), baseball - the Washington Nationals, basketball - the Washington Wizards (men's) and the Washington Mystics (women's), and hockey - the Washington Capitals.

I could continue listing all of the parks, universities, historical buildings, shopping districts, restaurants, and entertainment venues in the DC area but this guidebook is supposed to be about Charlottesville, so I'll stop while I'm ahead. Anyway, I think you get the picture - there's more than a lot to do in Washington D.C.!

54. VIRGINIA BEACH

When I mentioned that you could easily get to the beach from C-ville for a weekend getaway, I wasn't lying. Virginia Beach is around a three-hour drive from C-ville and serves as the prime beach vacation destination for locals.

Virginia Beach lies where the Chesapeake Bay meets the Atlantic Ocean and is Virginia's biggest city. A three-mile boardwalk stretches along its beach-lined oceanfront with hundreds of resorts, hotels, restaurants, and attractions along the way. The city is even listed in the Guinness Book of Records as having the longest pleasure beach in the world!

Every year the city hosts the East Coast Surfing Championships as well as the North American Sand Soccer Championship. The Virginia Aquarium & Marine Science Center exhibits ocean life, including sharks, manta rays, and sea turtles in globally themed habitats. Virginia Beach is also home to several state parks, long-protected beach areas, military bases, and numerous historic sites. The bayside First Landing State Park marks the 1607 arrival of the Jamestown colonists from England (more about that next).

From the lively oceanfront area to remote Sandbridge, the calming Chesapeake Bay to the bustling Town Center, or the eclectic ViBe creative district to the surrounding inland areas, the perfect weekend getaway awaits you at Virginia Beach. Surf's up brah!

55. THE HISTORIC TRIANGLE (JAMESTOWN, COLONIAL WILLIAMSBURG, AND YORKTOWN)

If you didn't get enough history from the former presidential homes surrounding C-ville, then head two hours east to Virginia's Historic Triangle, where three distinct places make up the birthplace of the United States.

If you want to visit each area in chronological order, then you would start with **Jamestown**, where the first English settlers arrived in 1607. A National Park Service and Preservation Site, Historic Jamestowne allows you to discover the first permanent settlement in the "New World." Walking tours provide insight into 17th-century Jamestown and the research conducted by the Jamestown Rediscovery team, including an introduction to the settlement and an overview of the archeology of James Fort. You can see archeology in action by checking out excavations in progress outside the fort, near the East Bulwark. Or you can sort through real artifacts from said excavations as one of the many hands-on learning activities offered at the Ed Shed.

The centerpiece attraction of the Historic Triangle is **Colonial Williamsburg**, the largest living history museum in the world. The 301 acres that make up this historic village feature iconic sites, working tradespeople, historic taverns, and two world-class art museums. Your admission ticket comes with interpreter-guided tours of the most iconic sites, including the Capitol, Governor's Palace, and Courthouse. It also grants you access to multiple programs throughout the day, including staged performances and musical recitals at the various playhouses and theaters.

After reading so much about Thomas Jefferson in this guide, how would you like to meet him? During your visit, you may come across Nation Builders portraying real historical figures who were associated with 18th-century Williamsburg, including Jefferson, George and Martha Washington, and Patrick Henry. As you make your way through this colonial capitol, you'll encounter expert tradespeople who will share their craft with you in their workspaces, gardens, yards, and at the newly expanded and updated Art

Museums of Colonial Williamsburg. You'll also be able to take advantage of the complimentary shuttle service and get discounts on carriage rides. After all, the entire village is one mile long and half a mile wide!

Colonial Williamsburg also has a plethora of dining choices as well as affiliated hotels and resorts, allowing visitors to stay within walking distance of all the action. With all the activities, sites, and performances going on at Colonial Williamsburg, not to mention the special evening programs and seasonal events, it's easy to see how a family could spend an entire weekend here alone.

Then there's **Yorktown**, where the last major battle of the American Revolution was fought in 1781. It was here that General George Washington and his army, along with allied French forces, besieged and defeated General Lord Cornwallis's British army, effectively ending the war. Explore the Yorktown Battlefield and discover what it took for the United States to finally gain independence. Then head over to the American Revolution Museum at Yorktown for a unique look at the lives of everyday people overtaken by revolutionary events. There are exhibits recounting the lives of individuals, a recreated Continental Army encampment, and a 1780s farm.

56. THEME PARKS (BUSCH GARDENS, WATER COUNTRY USA, AND KING'S DOMINION)

Calling all thrill seekers! If you're looking to spice up your vacation with some thrills and excitement, then pick one of the three theme parks near C-ville for a day of rides, entertainment, and all-around fun.

Busch Gardens is in the city of Williamsburg and not far from Colonial Williamsburg. In fact, the latter offers weekend combo passes that include Busch Gardens and Water Country so that you get equal doses of history and high-octane adventure. Some of the best rides in this park are the classic Loch Ness Monster - the world's only double interlocking loop roller coaster, Apollo's Chariot, which drops from 210 feet, and the new Pantheon - the world's fastest multi-launch roller coaster. On a hot day, you can cool off on the Le Scoot log flume, the white-water

Roman Rapids, or the exciting Escape from Pompeii. If you're in need of something a little more relaxing, try a scenic ride on the Busch Gardens Railway, the Rhine River Cruise, or the Skyride for a birds-eye view of the park. There are also plenty of kid-friendly rides and attractions throughout the park, including the Land of the Dragons and the Sesame Street Forest of Fun. In addition to the rides, this park also has live entertainment and seasonal themes throughout the year, such as Howl-O-Scream and Christmas Town. *(Est. drive time: 2 hrs.)*

Neighboring Busch Gardens is **Water Country USA**, Virginia's largest water park, and the perfect outing for a hot summer day. This park offers slides of varying thrill levels for all ages. A lot of the rides use innertubes, which allows you to ride with friends and family. Big Daddy Falls, Cutback Water Coaster, and Colossal Curl use rafts that fit up to four people. While there, make sure you check out the new Aquazoid Amped, featuring a special effects show, pulse-pounding music, and dynamic lighting effects all during a thrilling water ride. You can also test your courage on the drop slide Vanish Point or relax in the pools and lazy river of Rock-n-Roll Island. For the little kiddies, there are the H2O UFO and Cow-A-Bunga play areas. *(Est. drive time: 2 hrs.)*

Kings Dominion, located just north of Richmond, is slightly closer to C-ville and offers more than 60 rides as well as shows, attractions, kids' areas, and a waterpark during the summer months. Old-school roller coasters such as Anaconda and the wooden Grizzly are classics, whereas newer rides offer unbeatable thrills, such as Virginia's first 4D spin coaster Tumbili, and the Intimidator 305 - one of the tallest and fastest roller coasters on the East Coast. New in 2022 is Jungle X-pedition, an immersive experience exploring an ancient jungle civilization, and little ones can get their own thrills at Planet Snoopy, featuring the entire Peanuts gang. Included with admission during the summer is Soak City, a 20-acre waterpark with water slides, splash pads, a wave pool, a lazy river, cabanas, and Coconut Shores - a 45-foot multi-level play structure. And just like Busch Gardens, Kings Dominion offers shows and events all year long, including their immersive international celebration, Grand Carnival, and the children's favorite fall-time attraction, The Great Pumpkin Fest. There's also the fear-inducing Halloween Haunt, as well as the merry and festive wonderland of Winterfest. *(Est. drive time: 1 hr. 30 min.)*

57. LURAY CAVERNS

This natural wonder was discovered in 1878 but it dates back around 4 million years ago. Luray Caverns, located in the small town of Luray, is the largest caverns in the eastern US and offers tours along lit, paved walkways past towering formations and through rooms the size of cathedrals - some boasting ceilings as tall as 10 stories! Aside from the dripping stalactites and stalagmites, you'll also come across shimmering draperies, enchanting mirrored pools, and the Great Stalacpipe Organ, which is spread out over 3.5 acres and is recorded in the Guinness Book of World Records as the world's largest instrument! *(Est. drive time: 1 hr. 30 min.)*

Included with your Luray Caverns tickets are the nearby Car & Carriage Caravan Museum, Shenandoah Heritage Village, and Toy Town Junction, a collection of trains and toys from yesteryear. Also nearby but requiring an additional fee are the Rope Adventure Park and the Garden Maze - the largest Evergreen hedge maze in the Mid-Atlantic.

SOURCES

blueridgeballoon.com

boarsheadresort.com

bodosbagels.com

buschgardens.com/williamsburg/

charlottesville.gov/462/outdoor-pools-spray-grounds

charlottesvillealetrail.org

chilesfamilyorchards.com/carter-mountain-orchard/

colonialwilliamsburg.org

cvilledogwood.com

dairymarketcville.com

dwr.virginia.gov/lakes/

foxfieldraces.com

hamiltonsrestaurant.com

highland.org

historicjamestowne.org

ivyinnrestaurant.com

jeffersontheater.com

keswick.com

kingfamilyvineyards.com/polo/

kingsdominion.com

lightingofthelawn.com

luraycaverns.com

massresort.com

michietavern.com

monticello.org

montpelier.org

montpelierraces.org

nps.gov/shen

oakhurstinn.com

rivannarivercompany.com

rivannatrails.org

the-clifton.com

theparamount.net

tingpavilion.com

uvafralinartmuseum.virginia.edu

vagardenweek.org

virginiatheatrefestival.org

visitcharlottesville.org

visitvirginiabeach.com

watercountryusa.com

wintergreenresort.com

TOP REASONS TO BOOK THIS TRIP

History: With a plethora of historical homes and districts in and around Charlottesville, you will find yourself learning just as much about the nation's history as you will about the city itself.

Food & Wine: The restaurants and eateries in Charlottesville are some of the best in the region. And the area's robust wine industry is giving Napa Valley a run for its money. If you consider yourself a foodie, then consider C-ville your utopia!

The Great Outdoors: Surrounded by majestic mountains and a National Park at its doorstep, Charlottesville offers visitors an opportunity to get outside and bond with nature, no matter what time of year you go.

PACKING AND PLANNING TIPS

A Week before Leaving

- Arrange for someone to take care of pets and water plants.

- Email and Print important Documents.

- Get Visa and vaccines if needed.

- Check for travel warnings.

- Stop mail and newspaper.

- Notify Credit Card companies where you are going.

- Passports and photo identification is up to date.

- Pay bills.

- Copy important items and download travel Apps.

- Start collecting small bills for tips.

- Have post office hold mail while you are away.

- Check weather for the week.

- Car inspected, oil is changed, and tires have the correct pressure.

- Check airline luggage restrictions.

- Download Apps needed for your trip.

Right Before Leaving

- Contact bank and credit cards to tell them your location.

- Clean out refrigerator.

- Empty garbage cans.

- Lock windows.

- Make sure you have the proper identification with you.

- Bring cash for tips.

- Remember travel documents.

- Lock door behind you.

- Remember wallet.

- Unplug items in house and pack chargers.

- Change your thermostat settings.

- Charge electronics, and prepare camera memory cards.

READ OTHER GREATER THAN A TOURIST BOOKS

Greater Than a Tourist- California: 50 Travel Tips from Locals

Greater Than a Tourist- Salem Massachusetts USA: 50 Travel Tips from a Local by Danielle Lasher

Greater Than a Tourist United States: 50 Travel Tips from Locals

Greater Than a Tourist- St. Croix US Virgin Islands USA: 50 Travel Tips from a Local by Tracy Birdsall

Greater Than a Tourist- Montana: 50 Travel Tips from a Local by Laurie White

Children's Book: Charlie the Cavalier Travels the World by Lisa Rusczyk Ed. D.

CZYKPublishing.com

METRIC CONVERSIONS

TEMPERATURE

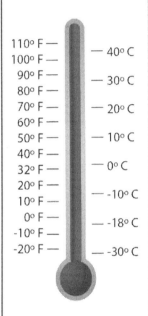

110° F	
100° F	— 40° C
90° F	— 30° C
80° F	
70° F	— 20° C
60° F	
50° F	— 10° C
40° F	
32° F	— 0° C
20° F	
10° F	— -10° C
0° F	— -18° C
-10° F	
-20° F	— -30° C

To convert F to C:

Subtract 32, and then multiply by 5/9 or .5555.

To Convert C to F:

Multiply by 1.8 and then add 32.

32F = 0C

LIQUID VOLUME

To Convert:......................Multiply by
U.S. Gallons to Liters................ 3.8
U.S. Liters to Gallons 26
Imperial Gallons to U.S. Gallons 1.2
Imperial Gallons to Liters....... 4.55
Liters to Imperial Gallons 22
1 Liter = .26 U.S. Gallon
1 U.S. Gallon = 3.8 Liters

DISTANCE

To convert ....Multiply by
Inches to Centimeters 2.54
Centimeters to Inches 39
Feet to Meters........................ .3
Meters to Feet 3.28
Yards to Meters 91
Meters to Yards 1.09
Miles to Kilometers 1.61
Kilometers to Miles............ .62
1 Mile = 1.6 km
1 km = .62 Miles

WEIGHT

1 Ounce = .28 Grams
1 Pound = .4555 Kilograms
1 Gram = .04 Ounce
1 Kilogram = 2.2 Pounds

107

TRAVEL QUESTIONS

- Do you bring presents home to family or friends after a vacation?

- Do you get motion sick?

- Do you have a favorite billboard?

- Do you know what to do if there is a flat tire?

- Do you like a sun roof open?

- Do you like to eat in the car?

- Do you like to wear sun glasses in the car?

- Do you like toppings on your ice cream?

- Do you use public bathrooms?

- Did you bring a cell phone and does it have power?

- Do you have a form of identification with you?

- Have you ever been pulled over by a cop?

- Have you ever given money to a stranger on a road trip?

- Have you ever taken a road trip with animals?

- Have you ever gone on a vacation alone?

- Have you ever run out of gas?

- If you could move to any place in the world, where would it be?

- If you could travel anywhere in the world, where would you travel?

- If you could travel in any vehicle, which one would it be?

- If you had three things to wish for from a magic genie, what would they be?

- If you have a driver's license, how many times did it take you to pass the test?

- What are you the most afraid of on vacation?

- What do you want to get away from the most when you are on vacation?

- What foods smell bad to you?

- What item do you bring on ever trip with you away from home?

- What makes you sleepy?

- What song would you love to hear on the radio when you're cruising on the highway?

- What travel job would you want the least?

- What will you miss most while you are away from home?

- What is something you always wanted to try?

- What is the best road side attraction that you ever saw?

- What is the farthest distance you ever biked?

- What is the farthest distance you ever walked?

- What is the weirdest thing you needed to buy while on vacation?

- What is your favorite candy?

- What is your favorite color car?

- What is your favorite family vacation?

- What is your favorite food?

- What is your favorite gas station drink or food?

- What is your favorite license plate design?

- What is your favorite restaurant?

- What is your favorite smell?

- What is your favorite song?

- What is your favorite sound that nature makes?

- What is your favorite thing to bring home from a vacation?

- What is your favorite vacation with friends?

- What is your favorite way to relax?

- Where is the farthest place you ever traveled in a car?

- Where is the farthest place you ever went North, South, East and West?

- Where is your favorite place in the world?

- Who is your favorite singer?

- Who taught you how to drive?

- Who will you miss the most while you are away?

- Who if the first person you will contact when you get to your destination?

- Who brought you on your first vacation?

- Who likes to travel the most in your life?

- Would you rather be hot or cold?

- Would you rather drive above, below, or at the speed limited?

- Would you rather drive on a highway or a back road?

- Would you rather go on a train or a boat?

- Would you rather go to the beach or the woods?

TRAVEL BUCKET LIST

1.

2.

3.

4.

5.

6.

7.

8.

9.

10.

NOTES

Made in the USA
Middletown, DE
05 July 2023